ROSY BOAS PETS

Understanding Habitat, Feeding, Handling, Breeding, Morphs, Lifespan, Health, Behavior, Temperature, Humidity, Lighting, Heating, Lifecycle, Enclosure, Diet, Supplements, Interaction.

Ethan Harry

Table of Contents

CHAPTER ONE

INTRODUCTION TO ROSY BOAS

Overview Of Rosy Boas

Rosy Boas are small, non-venomous snakes belonging to the family Boidae. They are celebrated for their gentle disposition and striking coloration, making them a popular choice among reptile enthusiasts. Typically, Rosy Boas reach lengths of 2 to 3 feet, with some individuals growing slightly larger. Their colors vary widely, ranging from shades of orange and brown to more muted grays and whites, often with distinct stripe patterns running down their bodies.

One of the most appealing aspects of Rosy Boas is their manageable size and calm nature, making them suitable for both novice and experienced snake keepers. They are generally easy to handle and rarely exhibit aggressive behavior, preferring to curl up when threatened rather than strike. This docile temperament, combined with their relatively simple care requirements, has made Rosy Boas a favorite in the pet trade.

In addition to their temperament and coloration, Rosy Boas are known for their adaptability to different environments. They thrive in a variety of habitats, from deserts to coastal areas, and their care in captivity reflects this versatility. Providing a suitable enclosure with proper temperature gradients, hiding spots, and a diet primarily consisting of appropriately sized rodents is essential for their well-being. Regular handling and interaction can help maintain their docile nature, making them a joy to keep and observe.

Rosy Boas are also relatively long-lived, with lifespan often exceeding 20 years when properly cared for. This longevity, coupled with their manageable size and ease of care, makes them an excellent choice for anyone looking to commit to a pet snake. Whether you are a seasoned herpetologist or a beginner, Rosy Boas offer a rewarding and fascinating experience as a pet, bringing a touch of the wild into your home while being easy to manage and care for.

Natural Habitat And Distribution

Rosy Boas (Lichanura trivirgata) are native to the southwestern United States and northwestern Mexico, inhabiting a variety of arid and semi-arid environments. Their natural range includes parts of California, Arizona, and Nevada in the U.S., as well as regions of Baja California and Sonora in Mexico. These snakes are typically found in rocky desert areas, scrublands, and coastal sage scrub habitats, where their distinct banded coloration provides excellent camouflage among the rocks and vegetation.

Adapted to survive in harsh, dry conditions, Rosy Boas often seek shelter during the day to escape the extreme heat. They utilize rocky crevices, burrows, and spaces under rocks to stay cool and protected. This behavior also helps them conserve moisture in their arid environments. As nocturnal hunters, they become more active at night, when temperatures are cooler, allowing them to search for prey. Their diet mainly consists of small mammals, such as rodents, but they also consume birds and lizards. This varied diet helps them thrive in diverse environments where food availability can be unpredictable.

The distribution of Rosy Boas is influenced by their need for specific habitat features, such as rocky terrains and scrublands that provide ample hiding spots and hunting grounds. In coastal sage scrub habitats, they benefit from the moderate climate and dense vegetation, which supports a healthy population of prey animals.

Rosy Boas' hardiness and adaptability to different environmental conditions contribute to their success both in the wild and in captivity. Their ability to thrive in captivity makes them popular among reptile enthusiasts. They are known for their docile nature, manageable size, and relatively simple care requirements, which makes them suitable pets for both novice and experienced keepers. The conservation of their natural habitats is essential to ensure the continued survival of Rosy Boas in the wild, as habitat destruction and fragmentation pose significant threats to their populations.

History And Domestication

The domestication of Rosy Boas as pets has a history stretching back several decades, with the first captive-bred individuals entering the pet trade in the mid-20th century. Early reptile enthusiasts were captivated by these snakes due to their manageable size, attractive appearance, and gentle temperament. Over time, selective breeding practices have yielded a variety of color morphs and patterns, enhancing their appeal and popularity within the reptile community.

In the wild, Rosy Boas are known for their resilience and ability to thrive in challenging environments. This inherent toughness, combined with their distinctive appearance, led to an increased interest in keeping them as pets. As more individuals began breeding Rosy Boas in captivity, the collective understanding of their care and husbandry improved significantly. This progress has resulted in healthier and more vibrant captive populations, benefiting both the snakes and their keepers.

Today, Rosy Boas are readily available in the pet trade, with many reputable breeders offering captive-bred specimens. The widespread availability of these captive-bred individuals has contributed to a decrease in the demand for wild-caught Rosy Boas, aiding in the conservation of natural populations. By opting for captive-bred snakes, pet owners support efforts to preserve wild populations and ensure the ongoing health of the species.

Keeping a Rosy Boa as a pet offers numerous benefits. For the owner, it provides the enjoyment of caring for and observing a fascinating reptile with unique behaviors and characteristics. Additionally, the purchase of captive-bred Rosy Boas supports ethical breeding practices and contributes to the overall well-being of the species. Through responsible ownership and continued education about their care, Rosy Boas can thrive in captivity, bringing joy to their owners and helping to preserve their presence in the wild.

Benefits Of Keeping A Rosy Boa As A Pet

Keeping a Rosy Boa as a pet offers numerous benefits that make them an excellent choice for reptile enthusiasts of all experience levels. One of their standout advantages is their gentle and docile nature, which makes them exceptionally easy to handle and interact with. Unlike some other snake species, Rosy Boas are not prone to biting and are generally tolerant of being handled by their owners.

In addition to their temperament, Rosy Boas have relatively low maintenance requirements. They do not need large enclosures, making them suitable for individuals with limited space. A simple setup with appropriate heating, humidity levels, and hiding spots is sufficient to maintain their health and happiness. Their diet is straightforward as well, primarily consisting of appropriately sized rodents, which are readily available from pet stores or breeders.

Another significant benefit of keeping a Rosy Boa is their long lifespan. Many individuals can live 20 years or more in captivity with proper care, allowing owners to form lasting bonds and enjoy years of companionship. Furthermore, Rosy Boas come in a variety of color morphs and patterns, ensuring there's a boa to suit every aesthetic preference.

Beyond their companionship and aesthetic appeal, Rosy Boas provide a rewarding educational experience. Observing their behaviors and learning about their natural history can deepen one's appreciation for these fascinating reptiles. For families, owning a Rosy Boa can be an engaging way to teach children about responsibility, biology, and the importance of conservation efforts aimed at preserving their natural habitats.

☐

CHAPTER TWO

CHOOSING YOUR ROSY BOA

Selecting A Healthy Rosy Boa

When selecting a Rosy Boa, ensuring the snake's health should be your primary concern. Start by observing its activity and alertness; a healthy Rosy Boa will be curious and responsive to its surroundings. Check its eyes, which should be clear and free of any cloudiness or discharge. The snake's body should be firm and well-muscled, indicating proper nutrition and overall well-being.

Respiratory health is crucial, so listen for any wheezing or look for bubbles around the nostrils, as these can be signs of respiratory distress. Inspect the snake's skin for external parasites, such as mites, which appear as small black or red dots.

Another indicator of good health is the snake's shedding process. Healthy Rosy Boas will shed their skin in one piece, and there should be no remnants stuck around sensitive areas like the eyes or tail.

Examine the snake's belly for any signs of scale rot or lesions, which might suggest it has been kept in unsanitary conditions. These signs include discoloration, swelling, or open sores on the underside of the snake. A consistent feeding history is also essential. Inquire about the snake's feeding schedule and request records from the seller. A well-fed Rosy Boa should not look overly thin or emaciated; it should have a slightly rounded body without prominent spine or ribs.

If possible, observe the snake during feeding to ensure it eats regularly and without issues. A consistent appetite is a good sign of health. By thoroughly inspecting these aspects, you can select a Rosy Boa that is healthy and ready to thrive in its new home. Prioritizing these checks will help ensure that your new pet is in good health and will remain a delightful companion for years to come.

Understanding Morphs And Color Variations

Rosy Boas are renowned for their diverse morphs and color variations, making them a popular choice among snake enthusiasts. Morphs refer to the genetic variations that produce different colors and patterns in these snakes, adding to their visual appeal. Among the most common morphs are the Coastal Rosy Boa, Desert Rosy Boa, and the Mexican Rosy Boa, each showcasing distinct color patterns and markings.

The Coastal Rosy Boa is typically characterized by a grayish-blue base color adorned with orange or reddish stripes. This morph is particularly striking due to its contrasting hues, making it a favorite for many collectors. The Desert Rosy Boa, on the other hand, usually displays a lighter background color, ranging from cream to light brown, with darker stripes running along its body. This subtle yet elegant color scheme allows it to blend seamlessly into its native arid habitats. The Mexican Rosy Boa, known for its vibrant and high-contrast patterns, exhibits a wide range of colors, making it one of the most visually diverse morphs available.

When selecting a morph, it is essential to consider both aesthetic preferences and budget constraints. While some morphs, like the Coastal and Desert varieties, may be more readily available and affordable, others, such as certain Mexican morphs, can be rarer and more expensive due to their unique and striking appearances. The rarity and demand for specific morphs can significantly influence their price, so it's crucial to research and choose a morph that aligns with both your visual preferences and financial capacity.

In addition to their beauty, understanding the genetic background and care requirements of each morph can enhance the overall experience of keeping a Rosy Boa. By choosing a morph that captivates you and fits within your budget, you can enjoy the rewarding experience of owning one of these fascinating and visually stunning snakes.

Where To Buy: Breeders Vs. Pet Stores

Deciding where to purchase your Rosy Boa is a crucial step in ensuring you get a healthy, well-adjusted snake. Both breeders and pet stores have their own set of pros and cons that you should consider before making a decision.

Breeders are often considered the best choice for acquiring a Rosy Boa. They usually possess specialized knowledge and experience, which allows them to provide detailed information about the snake's lineage, health history, and specific care requirements. Breeders typically breed their snakes in controlled environments, ensuring optimal conditions that promote the health and well-being of the animals. This attention to detail often results in snakes that are well-adjusted and accustomed to human interaction. Furthermore, buying from a reputable breeder can give you peace of mind knowing that the snake has been raised with proper care and attention to its needs.

On the other hand, pet stores offer the convenience of location and immediate availability. This can be especially appealing if you are looking to purchase a Rosy Boa quickly without waiting for a breeder's availability. However, the conditions in which the snakes are kept can vary widely between stores. Some pet stores may not have staff knowledgeable about the specific needs of Rosy Boas, which can lead to inadequate care and potentially unhealthy animals. It's essential to choose a pet store with a good reputation for animal care if you decide to go this route. Look for stores that keep their animals in clean, spacious enclosures and have staff who can answer questions about the snake's care and health.

Questions To Ask The Seller

When purchasing a Rosy Boa, asking the seller the right questions is crucial to ensure you make an informed decision. Here are some key questions to consider, along with their significance:

1.   How old is the Rosy Boa?

Knowing the age of the Rosy Boa is essential because it helps you understand the life stage the snake is in. Younger snakes may require different care and feeding schedules compared to older ones. Additionally, age can influence the snake's behavior and health needs.

2.   What is the snake's feeding schedule?

Understanding the feeding habits and schedule of the Rosy Boa is vital for maintaining consistency in its diet. Ask the seller how often the snake is fed, what type of food it prefers, and if it has any specific dietary requirements. This information helps you prepare for the snake's nutritional needs and ensures a smooth transition to its new environment.

3.   Has the snake had any health issues?

Inquiring about the Rosy Boa's health history can give you insights into potential future health problems and how to prepare for them. Ask the seller if the snake has had any past illnesses, injuries, or health conditions. Knowing this can help you take preventive measures and ensure the snake receives appropriate care.

4. What is the snake's temperament?

The temperament of the Rosy Boa is an important factor to consider. Ask the seller about the snake's general behavior and temperament. Is it docile and easy to handle, or does it tend to be more aggressive? This information can help you determine if the snake is a good fit for your household and experience level with reptiles.

5. Can I see records of veterinary visits?

Requesting records of veterinary visits ensures that the Rosy Boa has received proper medical care. These records can provide information on vaccinations, treatments, and overall health status.

Reviewing veterinary records can give you peace of mind and help you make an informed decision about the purchase.

By asking these questions, you can gather essential information about the Rosy Boa, ensuring that you are well-prepared to provide it with the best possible care.

CHAPTER THREE

HOUSING AND ENVIRONMENT

Setting Up The Enclosure

Creating a suitable enclosure for your Rosy Boa is crucial for its health and well-being. The enclosure should be secure, spacious, and easy to maintain. A glass terrarium with a secure lid is a popular choice, as it allows you to monitor your snake while providing adequate ventilation. For a single Rosy Boa, a 20-gallon tank is sufficient, but larger is always better. Ensure the enclosure has a secure locking mechanism to prevent escapes.

When setting up the enclosure, consider the natural habitat of Rosy Boas, which are native to arid and semi-arid regions. Mimicking their natural environment helps reduce stress and promote natural behaviors. Include plenty of horizontal space for your Rosy Boa to explore and hide. Providing multiple hiding spots is essential, as these snakes are known for their secretive nature. Hides can be made from commercially available products or simple items like overturned flower pots or small cardboard boxes. Ensure that the hides are snug and secure, giving your Rosy Boa a sense of safety.

The substrate is another critical aspect of the enclosure setup. Choose a substrate that retains some moisture but dries out quickly, such as aspen shavings or cypress mulch. Avoid substrates like cedar or pine, as these can be toxic to reptiles. The substrate should be deep enough to allow your Rosy Boa to burrow, as they often enjoy doing so.

Maintaining proper temperature and humidity levels is vital for your Rosy Boa's health. Provide a temperature gradient within the enclosure, with a warm side and a cooler side. The warm side should be around 85-90°F, while the cooler side should be around 75-80°F. Use a heat mat or a ceramic heat emitter to achieve the desired temperatures, and always use a thermostat to prevent overheating. Humidity levels should be kept between 40-60%, with occasional misting if necessary.

Lastly, provide a shallow water dish that is large enough for your Rosy Boa to soak in. Fresh water should be available at all times and changed regularly to prevent bacterial growth. By following these guidelines, you can create a comfortable and healthy environment for your Rosy Boa, ensuring it thrives in captivity.

Substrate Options

Selecting the right substrate, or bedding material, for your Rosy Boa's enclosure is crucial for its comfort and hygiene. Several substrate options are available, each with its own advantages and disadvantages.

Aspen Shavings are a popular choice among Rosy Boa owners. These shavings are easy to clean and allow the snake to burrow, mimicking its natural behavior. Aspen is also relatively dust-free, which is beneficial for the snake's respiratory health. However, it's important to avoid pine or cedar shavings, as they contain oils that can be harmful to reptiles.

Coconut Husk Fiber is another excellent option. This substrate helps maintain proper humidity levels in the enclosure, which is crucial for the snake's skin health, especially during shedding. Coconut husk fiber is also safe if ingested in small amounts and is biodegradable and eco-friendly. It provides a more naturalistic environment, making it a popular choice for creating a habitat that closely resembles the snake's natural surroundings.

Reptile Carpet is a reusable and easy-to-clean substrate. It can be a cost-effective option over time, as it doesn't need to be replaced as frequently as other substrates. However, it's essential to clean and disinfect the carpet regularly to prevent bacterial growth. Reptile carpet does not support burrowing, so it may not be suitable for all snakes.

Paper Towels or Newspaper are the most economical and straightforward substrates. They are particularly useful in quarantine or medical setups due to their ease of replacement and the ability to monitor waste and health issues closely. However, they do not provide a naturalistic environment and do not support burrowing behaviors, making them less ideal for long-term use in a display enclosure.

Temperature And Humidity Requirements

Maintaining proper temperature and humidity levels in the enclosure is essential for your Rosy Boa's health. These snakes require a temperature gradient to regulate their body temperature effectively. The warm side of the enclosure should be maintained between 85-90°F (29-32°C), while the cool side should be kept between 75-80°F (24-27°C). It's crucial to use a reliable thermometer to monitor temperatures at both ends of the enclosure to ensure the environment stays within these ranges.

To provide a suitable basking spot, use a heat source such as a heat lamp or an under-tank heater. It's important to regulate the heat source with a thermostat to prevent the risk of overheating, which can be harmful to your Rosy Boa. Avoid using hot rocks, as they can become excessively hot and cause burns to your snake.

In addition to temperature, maintaining appropriate humidity levels is vital for the health of your Rosy Boa. These snakes thrive in relatively low humidity, between

30-40%. Higher humidity levels can lead to respiratory issues, so it's important to keep the environment dry. To monitor humidity levels, use a hygrometer and make adjustments as needed. Adequate ventilation is also essential to prevent the growth of mold and mildew, which can be detrimental to your snake's health.

Ensure that the enclosure has proper ventilation to maintain a healthy airflow, which will help keep humidity levels in check and reduce the risk of respiratory problems. If necessary, you can use dehumidifiers or increase ventilation to achieve the desired humidity levels. By closely monitoring and adjusting the temperature and humidity, you can create an optimal environment that supports the health and well-being of your Rosy Boa.

Lighting And Heating

While Rosy Boas do not require UVB lighting like some reptiles, providing a consistent day-night cycle is highly beneficial for their well-being. A regular light cycle helps regulate their biological clock, contributing to their overall health and activity levels. To achieve this, you can use a standard incandescent bulb or a low-wattage reptile bulb to provide light during the day. Aim for a 12-hour light and 12-hour dark cycle, mimicking their natural environment and promoting a healthy routine.

When it comes to heating, a combination of heat lamps and under-tank heaters is essential to create an optimal environment for your Rosy Boa. Heat lamps are effective for providing basking spots, while under-tank heaters help maintain a stable temperature gradient within the enclosure. It is crucial to place heat sources outside the enclosure or ensure they are securely guarded to prevent accidental burns to your snake.

Position heat mats under one side of the tank to establish a temperature gradient, allowing your Rosy Boa to thermoregulate by moving between warmer and cooler areas as needed. This gradient is vital for their digestion and overall metabolic processes. Maintaining an appropriate temperature range is crucial, with a basking spot temperature around 90°F and a cooler side around 75°F. These conditions replicate the natural habitat of Rosy Boas, promoting their health and activity.

To ensure the safety and effectiveness of your heating setup, always use a reliable thermostat to regulate heat sources. A thermostat helps prevent overheating, which can be detrimental to your Rosy Boa's health. Regular monitoring of temperatures within the enclosure is also important to maintain a consistent and suitable environment. By providing a well-regulated lighting and heating system, you can create a comfortable and safe habitat for your Rosy Boa, supporting their well-being and longevity.

Creating Hiding Spots And Enrichment

Providing hiding spots and environmental enrichment is crucial for the mental and physical health of your Rosy Boa. Hiding spots help reduce stress by offering your snake a secure place to retreat. It's essential to place multiple hides in both the warm and cool areas of the enclosure to allow your snake to thermoregulate while feeling safe. You can use commercial reptile hides or create your own using non-toxic materials like cardboard boxes or PVC pipes. Make sure the hides are appropriately sized for your snake to feel snug but not cramped.

Environmental enrichment involves incorporating elements that mimic your snake's natural habitat. This can include items like branches, rocks, and tunnels, which encourage exploration and natural behaviors such as climbing and burrowing. Ensure these items are securely placed to prevent them from falling and causing injury to your snake. For example, sturdy branches can provide climbing opportunities, while rocks can create natural hiding spots. Tunnels can be made from various materials, including cork bark or PVC pipes, offering additional areas for your snake to explore and hide.

Maintaining a clean and sanitized enclosure is also vital for your Rosy Boa's health. Regular spot cleaning should be done daily to remove waste and uneaten food. This helps prevent the buildup of harmful bacteria and keeps the enclosure hygienic. Additionally, replace the substrate as needed to ensure a clean and comfortable environment. A thorough cleaning of the entire enclosure, including all accessories, should be performed at least once a month. Use reptile-safe disinfectants to sanitize the enclosure and rinse thoroughly to remove any chemical residues.

CHAPTER FOUR

FEEDING AND NUTRITION

Understanding The Rosy Boa Diet

Rosy Boas are carnivorous reptiles that primarily feed on small mammals in the wild. In captivity, their diet usually consists of mice and small rats. It's essential to provide a diet that closely mimics what they would naturally eat to keep them healthy. Baby Rosy Boas, or hatchlings, typically start with pinky mice, which are newborn mice. As they grow, the size of the prey should increase accordingly. Adult Rosy Boas can handle adult mice or even small rats, depending on their size.

Feeding frequency is an important aspect of maintaining a healthy Rosy Boa. Hatchlings generally require food more frequently, about once a week, while adults may only need feeding every 10 to 14 days. Overfeeding can lead to obesity, which can cause various health issues such as fatty liver disease and reduced lifespan. Signs of obesity include a noticeably rounder body and rolls of fat near the tail. To prevent overfeeding, it's crucial to monitor the boa's body condition and adjust the feeding schedule accordingly.

Underfeeding, on the other hand, can result in malnutrition, leading to stunted growth, weakened immune system, and other health complications. A malnourished Rosy Boa may appear thin, with visible spine and ribs. In such cases, increasing the frequency or size of feedings may be necessary until the snake reaches a healthier condition.

When feeding Rosy Boas, it's advisable to offer pre-killed or frozen-thawed prey rather than live animals. This practice not only ensures the safety of the snake but also eliminates the risk of the prey injuring the boa. Additionally, it's important to provide fresh water at all times, as hydration plays a critical role in digestion and overall health.

Feeding Schedule And Portions

Understanding the feeding schedule and portions for Rosy Boas is crucial to maintaining their health and well-being. The frequency of feeding varies based on the snake's age and size. Hatchlings and juveniles, which are more active and growing rapidly, require more frequent meals. They should be fed once every 5 to 7 days. This frequent feeding ensures they receive the necessary nutrients for their rapid growth and energy needs.

As Rosy Boas mature, their growth rate slows, and their metabolism stabilizes. Consequently, the feeding frequency can be reduced. Adult Rosy Boas typically only need to be fed once every 10 to 14 days. This schedule aligns with their slower metabolism and reduced energy requirements. However, it is essential to monitor your snake's body condition regularly. If you notice your Rosy Boa gaining excessive weight or becoming too thin, you may need to adjust the feeding frequency accordingly. An overweight snake may require less frequent feeding, while an underweight snake might benefit from more frequent meals.

Portion size is another critical aspect of feeding Rosy Boas. The general rule of thumb is to offer prey items that are approximately the same width as the thickest part of your Rosy Boa's body. This guideline helps ensure that the prey is appropriately sized for the snake's digestive system, preventing potential issues like regurgitation. Feeding prey that is too large can lead to digestive problems, while prey that is too small may not provide adequate nutrition.

Monitoring and adjusting both the feeding schedule and portion sizes based on your Rosy Boa's condition and behavior are essential for their health. Consistently offering the right amount of food at appropriate intervals will contribute to the overall well-being of your Rosy Boa, ensuring they thrive in captivity.

Live Vs. Frozen/Thawed Prey

Feeding live prey versus frozen/thawed prey to your Rosy Boa is a topic of much discussion among snake enthusiasts. Each method has its own advantages and disadvantages, making the decision a matter of preference and priority for the snake owner.

Feeding live prey can be beneficial in several ways. It provides a more stimulating environment for your Rosy Boa, as the act of hunting and capturing live prey mimics their natural behavior in the wild. This can contribute to the snake's overall physical and mental well-being, offering an enriching activity that promotes natural instincts. However, there are significant risks associated with live prey. Mice and rats, when alive, have the potential to bite and injure your snake. These bites can lead to infections, abscesses, and other health issues that may require veterinary attention. Additionally, the stress of capturing and subduing live prey can be considerable for the snake.

On the other hand, frozen/thawed prey is widely regarded as the safer and more convenient option. Freezing prey kills off parasites and pathogens that could otherwise harm your Rosy Boa, providing a cleaner and more hygienic meal. From a practical standpoint, frozen/thawed prey is easier to store and can be bought in bulk, reducing the frequency of trips to the pet store. This method also eliminates the risk of injury to your snake, as the prey is already deceased. To properly feed frozen/thawed prey, it's crucial to ensure that the food is completely thawed and warmed to room temperature before offering it to your snake. This mimics the body temperature of live prey, making it more appealing to your Rosy Boa and easier to digest.

Supplements And Vitamins

Maintaining a proper diet for your Rosy Boa is crucial for its health and well-being. While a diet of appropriately sized mice and rats typically provides all the necessary nutrients, there are instances where supplements and vitamins may be beneficial.

One of the primary supplements to consider is calcium. Calcium is essential for many bodily functions, including bone health, muscle function, and nerve transmission. In the case of breeding females, the demand for calcium increases significantly. Ensuring adequate calcium intake is crucial for the development of healthy eggs and preventing conditions such as metabolic bone disease (MBD). Similarly, snakes recovering from illness or injury may benefit from additional calcium to support the healing process. Vitamin D3 is another important nutrient that aids in calcium absorption. While Rosy Boas can produce vitamin D3 through exposure to UVB light, providing a dietary source can be beneficial, especially for snakes that do not receive adequate UVB exposure. Multivitamin supplements can also be considered to ensure a balanced intake of essential vitamins and minerals.

If you suspect your Rosy Boa may need additional vitamins or supplements, it is essential to consult with a reptile veterinarian. They can assess your snake's health, diet, and environmental conditions to recommend specific products and dosages. Over-supplementation can be harmful, so professional guidance is crucial.

When selecting supplements, opt for products specifically formulated for reptiles. These are designed to meet the unique dietary needs of snakes and other reptiles. Follow the manufacturer's instructions carefully and monitor your snake for any signs of improvement or adverse reactions.

Hydration Needs

Hydration is a vital yet frequently overlooked aspect of your Rosy Boa's overall health. Ensuring your Rosy Boa has constant access to fresh, clean water is essential. A shallow water dish, large enough for your snake to soak in, should be provided in their enclosure. This soaking not only aids in hydration but also facilitates shedding, a critical process for your snake's well-being.

Your Rosy Boa's water dish should be monitored daily. This involves checking the water level and cleanliness to ensure it remains suitable for consumption and bathing. Regularly changing the water is necessary to prevent contamination. Stagnant or dirty water can harbor bacteria and parasites, posing a health risk to your snake.

In addition to drinking, Rosy Boas may also use their water dish for defecation or bathing. This behavior emphasizes the importance of maintaining a clean environment. Frequent inspections and cleanings of the water dish will help prevent any potential health issues. When cleaning, use a mild, reptile-safe disinfectant to ensure all harmful organisms are eliminated without leaving toxic residues.

It's important to note that the size and shape of the water dish are crucial. It should be shallow enough for the Rosy Boa to enter and exit easily but large enough to allow full-body soaking. This soaking can be particularly beneficial during the shedding process, as it helps loosen the old skin.

Observing your Rosy Boa's interaction with the water dish can provide insights into their hydration status. If you notice your snake frequently soaking or spending a lot of time in the water, it might indicate underlying issues such as mites or dehydration. In such cases, reassess the humidity levels in the enclosure and consult a reptile veterinarian if necessary.

CHAPTER FIVE

HEALTH AND WELLNESS

Common Health Issues

Rosy Boas, like all pets, are susceptible to a range of health issues, with respiratory infections being one of the most common. These infections often result from poor husbandry conditions such as low temperatures or high humidity. Symptoms to watch for include wheezing, mucus around the nose and mouth, and labored breathing. Prompt action is necessary to address these symptoms, as respiratory infections can quickly worsen if left untreated.

Another frequent issue is mouth rot, also known as infectious stomatitis. This condition is typically caused by bacteria that proliferate due to poor enclosure hygiene or an injury to the mouth. Signs of mouth rot include swelling around the mouth, the presence of pus, and a reluctance to eat. Maintaining a clean enclosure and promptly treating any injuries can help prevent mouth rot, but once it occurs, veterinary intervention is crucial to clear the infection and prevent further complications.

Scale rot is another bacterial infection that can affect Rosy Boas. This condition is often the result of unsanitary living conditions, where bacteria thrive and infect the skin. Scale rot can be identified by discolored, damaged, or ulcerated scales, which may also emit a foul odor. Ensuring the enclosure is clean and dry is essential in preventing scale rot. If detected, treatment involves cleaning the affected area and sometimes administering antibiotics under the guidance of a veterinarian.

Digestive problems are also a concern and can arise from feeding inappropriate food or from stress. Symptoms of digestive issues include regurgitation of food, a lack of appetite, or abnormal stools. Providing a proper diet and reducing stressors in the environment are key preventive measures. Regular monitoring of eating habits and stool quality can help in early detection and treatment of digestive problems.

Signs Of A Healthy Rosy Boa

Understanding the characteristics of a healthy Rosy Boa is crucial for early problem detection. Firstly, observe the eyes of your Rosy Boa. Healthy Rosy Boas have clear, bright eyes devoid of any discharge or cloudiness. This clarity is a strong indicator of overall health and vitality.

Next, examine the skin of your Rosy Boa. It should be smooth and shiny, reflecting proper hydration and good nutrition. There should be no cuts, scrapes, sores, or signs of skin infections. Any irregularities in the skin can indicate underlying health issues that need to be addressed promptly.

A healthy Rosy Boa will exhibit a strong feeding response. This means that it will readily eat its prey, indicating a good appetite and proper metabolic function. A lack of interest in food over an extended period can signal health concerns that may require veterinary attention.

Activity levels are also a key indicator of health. Healthy Rosy Boas are active and curious, particularly during their active periods. They should move smoothly without any signs of wobbling, lethargy, or difficulty. A well-moving snake is usually a healthy snake.

Regular and well-formed feces are another sign of a healthy Rosy Boa. Proper digestion and regular bowel movements indicate that the digestive system is functioning correctly. Keep an eye out for changes in fecal consistency, frequency, or the presence of parasites.

Veterinary Care

Regular veterinary care is crucial for maintaining the health of your Rosy Boa. Finding a veterinarian experienced with reptiles is essential, as they will be familiar with the specific needs and issues that these snakes can face. A reptile-savvy vet can provide expert guidance on proper care and address any health concerns specific to Rosy Boas.

Annual check-ups are highly recommended to catch any potential health issues early. During these visits, the vet will typically conduct a comprehensive physical examination to assess the overall health of your Rosy Boa. They will check for common problems such as mites, respiratory infections, and skin issues. Additionally, the vet may recommend routine fecal exams to check for internal parasites, which can often go unnoticed but can significantly impact your snake's health.

Blood tests and other diagnostics might be advised if any concerns arise during the examination. These tests can provide valuable insights into your Rosy Boa's internal health, helping to identify issues such as metabolic bone disease or nutritional deficiencies. Early detection of health problems is vital for effective treatment and can prevent more serious complications.

Between veterinary visits, it is important to monitor your Rosy Boa closely for any signs of illness. Keep an eye on its behavior and physical condition. If you notice any changes, such as refusal to eat, lethargy, abnormal discharge, or difficulty shedding, seek veterinary care immediately. Prompt attention to these symptoms can make a significant difference in the outcome of your Rosy Boa's health.

Parasite Prevention And Treatment

Parasites pose a significant threat to reptiles, including Rosy Boas, and addressing these issues is crucial for maintaining their health. Both external and internal parasites can afflict these snakes, leading to various health problems and discomfort.

External parasites, such as mites and ticks, are common culprits. Mites often appear as tiny black or red specks that move across the snake's skin, causing irritation and stress. Ticks, though less common, can also attach to the snake and feed on its blood, leading to potential infections. Preventing these infestations involves maintaining a clean and hygienic enclosure. Regular cleaning routines, proper substrate management, and ensuring that the enclosure is free from excess moisture can significantly reduce the risk of parasite proliferation. Additionally, it is essential to inspect your Rosy Boa regularly for any signs of mites or ticks. Quarantining new snakes before introducing them to your existing collection is another effective preventive measure, as it helps to avoid cross-contamination.

If an infestation is detected, several treatments are available. Reptile-safe sprays can be used to treat the snake and its enclosure. It's crucial to choose products specifically designed for reptiles to avoid harmful side effects. In more severe cases, a veterinarian might prescribe medication to eliminate the parasites.

Internal parasites, such as worms, also pose a threat to Rosy Boas. These parasites can be more challenging to detect as they live within the snake's digestive system. Symptoms of internal parasitic infections include weight loss, diarrhea, and regurgitation. Regular veterinary check-ups and fecal exams are essential to identify and address these issues promptly. If internal parasites are detected, deworming treatments prescribed by a vet can effectively manage and eliminate them.

Shedding Problems And Solutions

Shedding is a natural and vital process for Rosy Boas, allowing them to grow and maintain healthy skin. However, they can sometimes face difficulties shedding, a condition known as dysecdysis. This issue can arise due to various factors, including inadequate humidity, dehydration, or underlying health problems.

To ensure your Rosy Boa sheds properly, maintaining the right humidity levels in their enclosure is crucial. Typically, providing a humidity hide can achieve this. A humidity hide is a small, enclosed space filled with damp sphagnum moss, creating a microenvironment with higher humidity levels. Additionally, regular misting of the enclosure can help maintain appropriate humidity, benefiting the shedding process.

Signs of shedding difficulties include retained skin, particularly around the eyes or tail tip. If you notice your Rosy Boa struggling with retained skin, you can assist by gently soaking the snake in lukewarm water for about 15-20 minutes. This soaking can help loosen the retained skin, making it easier for the snake to shed completely. During this process, it's essential to handle your snake gently to avoid causing stress or injury.

CHAPTER SIX

HANDLING AND BEHAVIOR

Safe Handling Techniques

Handling a Rosy Boa safely is crucial to ensure the well-being of both the snake and the handler. When handling your Rosy Boa, always support its entire body to make it feel secure. Use both hands to gently scoop up the snake, approaching it slowly from the side rather than from above to avoid startling it. This approach minimizes stress and creates a more comfortable experience for the snake.

It's important to avoid sudden movements and loud noises when handling a Rosy Boa, as these can cause unnecessary stress. When lifting the snake, support its body along its entire length. This helps prevent any accidental injury and ensures the snake feels secure in your hands. Never grab the snake by its tail or head, as this can cause harm and provoke defensive behavior. Grabbing the tail can lead to tail breakage, while grabbing the head can cause the snake to feel threatened and bite in self-defense.

When the snake is moving through your hands, let it glide naturally without restricting its movement. This allows the Rosy Boa to explore its surroundings and feel more at ease. Regular handling helps the snake become more accustomed to human interaction, making future handling sessions easier and less stressful for both the handler and the snake.

Creating a positive handling experience is key to building trust with your Rosy Boa. Consistent, gentle handling will help the snake feel more comfortable and reduce any potential stress or defensive reactions. Always handle your Rosy Boa in a calm and quiet environment, free from sudden disturbances.

Understanding Rosy Boa Behavior

Understanding Rosy Boa behavior is essential for providing them with the best care. These snakes are generally known for their calm and docile nature, making them popular pets among reptile enthusiasts. In the wild, Rosy Boas are crepuscular, meaning they are most active during the twilight hours of dawn and dusk. During these times, they engage in hunting and exploring their surroundings. This natural behavior is crucial for their survival, as it helps them avoid the heat of the day and the cold of the night.

In captivity, Rosy Boas often retain these crepuscular habits. They spend considerable time burrowing or hiding under rocks and logs, mimicking their natural habitat. Providing ample hiding spots in their enclosure is vital. This can include rocks, logs, and specially designed hide boxes that can offer a sense of security. A well-structured environment helps reduce stress, contributing to the overall health and well-being of the snake.

Rosy Boas also have a strong feeding response, typically observed during their active periods. Understanding and observing these feeding behaviors can help owners determine the best times to offer food. Generally, it's best to feed them during the evening when they are naturally more active. Regular feeding schedules that align with their natural behavior can enhance their feeding response and ensure they receive the necessary nutrition.

Observing your Rosy Boa's behavior closely is key to understanding its needs and preferences. For instance, if a Rosy Boa is frequently burrowing or hiding, it might indicate a need for more hiding spots or adjustments in the enclosure temperature. On the other hand, a lack of activity might suggest health issues or environmental stress.

Socialization And Interaction

Socializing a Rosy Boa involves gentle and consistent interaction to help them become comfortable with human presence. Though these snakes are naturally solitary, regular handling can make them more relaxed around people. Begin with short handling sessions of a few minutes, gradually increasing the duration as your snake gets used to you. Handling sessions should always be calm and positive to ensure the snake associates the experience with safety and comfort.

When handling your Rosy Boa, avoid doing so immediately after feeding, as this can lead to regurgitation. Snakes need time to digest their meals undisturbed. Additionally, refrain from handling your snake if it is in shed. During shedding, snakes are more sensitive and may be more prone to stress. Their vision can also be impaired, making them more defensive and less tolerant of handling.

It's crucial to observe your snake's body language during handling sessions. Signs of stress include the snake tensing up, trying to escape, or displaying defensive behaviors such as hissing or striking. If your Rosy Boa exhibits any of these signs, it's best to end the handling session and give your snake a break. Consistent, gentle handling can help reduce stress over time, but it's important to respect your snake's limits and needs.

Gradually increasing the length of handling sessions can help your Rosy Boa build trust and familiarity. Patience is key; forcing interaction can lead to more stress and setbacks in socialization. Over time, with regular, calm, and gentle handling, your Rosy Boa can become more relaxed and comfortable with human interaction, making them a more enjoyable pet to have.

Stress Signs And How To Mitigate Them

Recognizing stress signs in Rosy Boas is essential for maintaining their health and well-being. Common indicators of stress include refusal to eat, frequent hiding, and excessive defensive behaviors, such as hissing or striking. If you observe any of these behaviors, it's crucial to evaluate the snake's living conditions and handling routine to address potential sources of stress.

Improper environmental conditions are a primary cause of stress in Rosy Boas. Ensure that the enclosure has the correct temperature gradient, appropriate humidity levels, and sufficient hiding spots. A well-maintained habitat with these elements can significantly reduce stress and promote a sense of security.

Overhandling is another common stressor. While social interaction is beneficial for acclimating your snake to human presence, too much handling can overwhelm and stress the animal. Finding a balance is key, allowing the snake to feel secure without feeling overwhelmed by frequent interactions.

Providing a stable and consistent routine can also help mitigate stress. This includes adhering to a regular feeding schedule, maintaining a clean enclosure, and ensuring the snake has a quiet, undisturbed area to retreat to when needed. Stability in their environment helps Rosy Boas feel safe and secure, reducing the likelihood of stress-related behaviors.

If stress signs persist despite optimizing their environment and handling routine, consulting a reptile veterinarian is advisable. A vet can help identify any underlying health issues that might be contributing to the snake's stress and provide further guidance on care and handling practices. They can also offer insights into specific needs that your Rosy Boa might have, ensuring comprehensive care and reducing stress effectively.

CHAPTER SEVEN

BREEDING ROSY BOAS

Understanding Breeding Behavior

Understanding the breeding behavior of Rosy Boas is fundamental to successful breeding efforts. These snakes exhibit specific mating habits, typically occurring in the spring following a period of brumation. Brumation is akin to hibernation in reptiles, where the animals experience a significant drop in temperature and a marked reduction in activity. This period is critical as it helps trigger the breeding season once temperatures rise again, signaling the end of brumation.

During the breeding season, male Rosy Boas engage in distinct courtship behaviors to attract females. One of the most noticeable behaviors is the male nudging the female, often aligning his body closely with hers. This physical alignment is a preliminary step in the courtship ritual, indicating the male's readiness to mate. Successful courtship often culminates in the male wrapping his body around the female, leading to copulation. This process can be quite prolonged, sometimes lasting several hours.

Observing these behaviors is essential for breeders. Recognizing when the snakes are ready to mate can help in timing the introduction of potential mates and ensuring optimal conditions for successful breeding. Additionally, understanding these natural behaviors can aid in creating an environment that mimics their natural habitat, which is conducive to breeding.

For instance, maintaining appropriate temperature fluctuations and ensuring a period of reduced activity can help simulate brumation, thereby triggering the breeding season.

Breeders should also be aware that not all courtship attempts lead to successful mating. It's important to monitor the interactions between the male and female, providing them with a stress-free environment. Patience and careful observation are key, as forcing or rushing the process can lead to unsuccessful breeding attempts and potentially stress the snakes.

Preparing For Breeding Season

Preparation is key to successful breeding for Rosy Boas. Start by ensuring that both the male and female Rosy Boas are healthy and of appropriate breeding age, typically around two to three years old. It's essential to provide a suitable environment that mimics their natural habitat, including proper temperature gradients, humidity levels, and hiding spots.

Begin the brumation process by gradually lowering the temperature in their enclosure to around 55-60°F (13-16°C) over a period of a few weeks. Maintain this temperature for about two to three months, then slowly raise it back to normal levels to signal the end of brumation. This cooling period is vital as it simulates the natural seasonal changes that trigger breeding.

During the breeding season, ensure that both snakes are well-fed and hydrated. Offering a varied diet of appropriately sized prey items will help maintain their health and energy levels. It's also important to monitor their behavior closely for signs of stress or illness.

Additionally, prepare a dedicated breeding enclosure that meets the needs of both snakes. This enclosure should include hiding spots, climbing branches, and a suitable substrate to mimic their natural environment. Ensure the enclosure is clean and free from parasites to provide a healthy breeding environment.

Monitor the snakes closely during the breeding season for signs of courtship behavior, such as increased activity and interaction between the male and female. It's important to provide a stress-free environment and avoid handling the snakes unnecessarily during this time.

Finally, after successful breeding, be prepared for the possibility of gravid (pregnant) females. Provide additional resources and care for gravid females, including increased food intake and a secure, comfortable environment for laying eggs.

Incubation And Hatchling Care

After successful copulation, the female Rosy Boa will develop eggs, with gestation lasting around four to six months. Providing optimal conditions during this period is crucial for the healthy development of the eggs. Create a secure and comfortable nesting area for the female, such as a simple hide filled with damp sphagnum moss or vermiculite to maintain humidity. Once the eggs are laid, carefully transfer them to an incubator set at a consistent temperature of 82-86°F (28-30°C) with high humidity.

Incubation typically takes about 60 to 70 days. During this time, avoid disturbing the eggs and maintain stable conditions within the incubator. As hatching approaches, keep an eye on the eggs but refrain from handling them. When the hatchlings start to emerge, they should be gently transferred to a separate enclosure designed to meet their needs.

Hatchling care involves setting up a suitable environment that includes a warm basking area, hiding spots, and a shallow water dish. Once the hatchlings have acclimated to their new surroundings, usually within a few days, offer appropriately sized prey such as pinky mice. Ensure the enclosure has a gradient of temperatures, allowing the hatchlings to regulate their body heat effectively.

Regular monitoring is essential to ensure the health and well-being of the young Rosy Boas. Gentle handling will help them become accustomed to human interaction, but be careful not to stress them with excessive handling. Keep an eye out for any signs of health issues and address them promptly to prevent complications.

Ethical Considerations

Breeding Rosy Boas entails significant ethical responsibilities to ensure the welfare of both adult snakes and their offspring. As a breeder, you must possess the requisite knowledge, resources, and commitment to provide comprehensive care for these snakes throughout their lives. This commitment involves understanding their dietary needs, habitat requirements, and health considerations to promote a thriving environment for the snakes.

Ethical breeding practices should prioritize the well-being of the snakes over profit or novelty. Breeding solely for financial gain or to produce rare morphs can lead to neglect of fundamental care responsibilities and compromise the snakes' health. Instead, the focus should be on enhancing the health and genetic diversity of Rosy Boas. This approach involves careful selection of breeding pairs to avoid inbreeding and promote robust genetic lines, which can contribute to the species' long-term vitality.

Preparedness to provide long-term care for any offspring is crucial. As a breeder, you must be ready to house and care for young snakes until they can be responsibly rehomed. Finding responsible homes for offspring involves vetting potential owners to ensure they have the capability and commitment to provide proper care. Educating new owners about the specific needs of Rosy Boas is part of your ethical duty to ensure the snakes' welfare continues beyond your care.

Legal and regulatory considerations are also essential in ethical breeding practices. Familiarize yourself with the local, state, and federal laws governing the breeding and selling of Rosy Boas. Compliance with these regulations not only ensures legal operation but also promotes responsible and sustainable breeding practices within the community.

CHAPTER EIGHT

ROSY BOA CARE AND MAINTENANCE

Daily Care Routines

Ensuring the health and happiness of your Rosy Boa involves simple yet essential daily care routines. Begin each day by monitoring the temperature and humidity levels in the enclosure. Rosy Boas thrive in temperatures ranging from 75-85°F during the day, with a slight drop at night. Humidity levels should be maintained between 40-60%. Adjust heating and humidity sources as needed to maintain these optimal conditions.

Next, inspect the enclosure for any signs of waste or leftover food. Promptly cleaning any messes helps prevent bacteria buildup and odor issues. This regular maintenance ensures a clean and healthy environment for your Rosy Boa. Additionally, providing fresh water daily is crucial for your pet's well-being. Replace the water in their dish each day to prevent the growth of harmful bacteria and to keep your snake hydrated.

Handling your Rosy Boa gently but regularly is important for maintaining its comfort with human interaction. Regular handling sessions allow you to check for any signs of health issues. During these interactions, observe your Rosy Boa for any unusual skin conditions, lethargy, or changes in appetite. A healthy Rosy Boa will exhibit clear eyes, a firm body, and a consistent appetite.

Weekly And Monthly Maintenance

In addition to daily routines, weekly and monthly maintenance tasks are crucial for maintaining a clean and safe environment for your Rosy Boa. Each week, undertake a thorough cleaning of the enclosure. This involves removing all substrate and decorations from the tank. Using a reptile-safe cleaner, disinfect the enclosure to eliminate any bacteria or parasites that may have accumulated. It is essential to allow the enclosure to dry completely before adding fresh substrate and returning the decorations.

A key part of weekly maintenance is checking the condition of the heating elements and lighting. Ensure these components are functioning correctly and providing the appropriate temperature gradient within the enclosure. The temperature gradient is vital for your Rosy Boa's health, allowing it to regulate its body temperature effectively. Any burnt-out bulbs or malfunctioning equipment should be replaced immediately to maintain a stable environment.

Monthly maintenance involves a more comprehensive examination of the entire setup. This includes inspecting and cleaning hides, water dishes, and climbing structures. These items can harbor bacteria and parasites if not cleaned regularly. Use a reptile-safe disinfectant to clean them thoroughly, ensuring all potential pathogens are eradicated.

If you use a natural substrate, it should be replaced completely every few months to prevent the buildup of waste and bacteria. This is important because over time, even with spot cleaning, waste can accumulate and create an unhealthy environment for your Rosy Boa.

Additionally, take this opportunity to reassess the overall condition of the enclosure. Check for any signs of wear or damage that might pose a risk to your pet. Regular maintenance not only ensures the health and well-being of your Rosy Boa but also helps in early detection of potential issues, allowing for prompt corrective action.

Long-Term Care Tips

Proper long-term care for your Rosy Boa is crucial to ensure its health and well-being. Start by consistently monitoring its growth through regular weighing and measuring. This helps you track its development and determine when adjustments in its care are necessary. As your Rosy Boa grows, it will need larger meals and possibly a more spacious enclosure. Typically, adult Rosy Boas should be fed every 10-14 days, while younger snakes might require more frequent feeding.

Shedding is a natural and important process for Rosy Boas. A healthy Rosy Boa should shed its skin in one complete piece. Pay close attention to its shedding cycles; incomplete sheds can signal health issues or inadequate humidity levels. To assist with shedding, slightly increase the humidity and provide a moist hide for your snake. This will help ensure that it can shed its skin properly.

Regular veterinary check-ups are essential for maintaining your Rosy Boa's health. Find a veterinarian experienced with reptiles to conduct these check-ups. They can identify potential health issues early and offer expert advice on proper care practices. Stay proactive by keeping up with the latest care recommendations and adjusting your practices as needed to provide the best care for your pet.

In addition to these measures, ensure your Rosy Boa's environment remains suitable for its needs. This includes maintaining appropriate temperature and humidity levels, providing a clean and safe enclosure, and offering enrichment opportunities to promote natural behaviors. By staying attentive to your Rosy Boa's needs and adapting its care over time, you can ensure a healthy, happy life for your pet. Regular monitoring, proper feeding, adequate shedding assistance, and veterinary care are all key components of successful long-term Rosy Boa care.

THE END

Made in United States
Troutdale, OR
04/11/2025

30530935R00056